Original title:
The Porcupine Principle

Copyright © 2024 Swan Charm
All rights reserved.

Editor: Jessica Elisabeth Luik
Author: Sebastian Sarapuu
ISBN HARDBACK: 978-9916-86-423-4
ISBN PAPERBACK: 978-9916-86-424-1

Spiny Nightwalkers

In the quiet dusk they roam,
Beneath the sky's velvet dome,
Spines aligned in moonlit glow,
Secrets whispered soft and low.

Shadows stretch and stars ignite,
Guiding steps through silver light,
Silent hunters of the night,
Nature's guardians out of sight.

Leaves rustle with each stride,
In the forest, side by side,
Echoes of an ancient song,
Spiny nightwalkers move along.

Wise old eyes survey the land,
Silent, steady, hand in hand,
Nocturnal dance in twilight's gleam,
Walking softly through a dream.

Underneath the midnight veil,
Stories of the earth prevail,
Footsteps fade with morning dew,
Nightwalkers vanish from the view.

Silent Defenders

In the night so calm and clear,
Shadowed figures standing near.
Armor donned for unseen fights,
Guardians of our fragile nights.

Whispers hushed by misted air,
Vigil kept with tender care.
Strength that roams in silent steps,
Safeguarding the dreams we kept.

Quills of Caution

In the silent twilight still,
Porcupine on the hill.
Needles ready to defend,
Trust not every friend.

Moonlight casts a guiding ray,
Danger looms, don't delay.
Sharp and steady armor worn,
In caution, brave is born.

Whispers of the forest deep,
Secrets porcupines keep.
Nature's gentle, yet may spurn,
In life's lessons, we learn.

Razor Plight

Beneath the moon's soft, silver glow,
A tale of sorrow, sharp and slow.
Paths entwined with destiny,
And edges keen with mystery.

With every step, a careful tread,
Through darkened trails that lie ahead.
Razor's plight in midnight's dance,
Entwined within a starry trance.

Touch of Thorn

A rose blooms with crimson grace,
Beauty hides a guarded face.
Petals soft, allure refined,
Thorns a shield, well-defined.

Touch with care, respect the might,
Blossoms hold their own light.
Defenses sharp, nature's charm,
Balance found in harm.

As the sun sets, shadows form,
Revealing the hidden thorn.
Life's embrace, both sweet and dire,
In each touch, spark and fire.

Spines of Strength

In a world of fleeting light,
Stands a form, both fierce and bright.
Bearing spines of ancient might,
To shield the weak through darkest night.

Roots that clasp the earth below,
Wisdom's whisper in winds that blow.
Strength resides within their stance,
Echoes of a timeless dance.

Defensive Elegance

Feathers preened with tender care,
Songs of night drift through the air.
Yet beneath, a strength concealed,
Beauty with defense revealed.

Wings unfold in graceful dance,
Nature's armor, bold stance.
Elegance in every line,
Protection's touch, divine.

Night's embrace, wisdom's flow,
In each movement, love will grow.
Defensive yet refined,
Elegance in strength defined.

Quilled Mystique

Moonlight weaves through shadows deep,
Where secrets in the stillness sleep.
Quills that guard a mystic keep,
In silence, ancient whispers seep.

Echoes of a time long past,
Reflected in the quills amassed.
Mystique that binds the night so tight,
A blend of dark and gentle light.

Prickly Paths

Through the desert, winds abide,
Cacti stand on every side.
Pathways paved with cautious steps,
Guardians of silent depths.

Sunrise paints a golden hue,
Journeys start anew.
Spines like soldiers, ever brave,
Mark the path nature gave.

Sand and spikes, a harsh disguise,
Strength unseen by human eyes.
Prickly paths, a tale they tell,
Of resilience where they dwell.

Barbed Embrace

In realms of shadow, thorny grace,
A tender touch, a barbed embrace,
Beneath the moon's reflective light,
Two souls entwine in silent night.

With whispered vows in gentle snare,
They weave a dance through midnight air,
Love's sharp edges, harsh yet sweet,
In passion's grip, their hearts shall meet.

Amidst the stars, their whispered dream,
A tapestry of hope, a gleam,
Intertwined, they face the fight,
Against the storms of endless night.

Whispers of Needles

Soft whispers through the needles sway,
A symphony in branches' play,
Where secrets drift in twilight's gaze,
Ensnared within the pine's embrace.

The forest hums a silent song,
Of tales of right, of tales of wrong,
An echo in the evening's breeze,
A mystery in whispering trees.

Glistening drops on needles lie,
Like tears that fall from frozen sky,
In nature's arms, the heart finds peace,
In whispers, silent sorrows cease.

Sheltered Wildness

In hidden glades, where shadows fall,
The wildness rests, beyond the call,
Of human sound or fleeting glance,
Within the forest's secret dance.

A world unseen by passing eyes,
Where nature's spirit softly flies,
Sheltered wildness claims its throne,
In silence, it is not alone.

Beneath the boughs, a haven found,
Where life in purest form's unbound,
A sanctuary, free, untamed,
In nature's heart, it stays unnamed.

Spiny Serenade

As dusk descends and shadows grow,
The cacti sing, a spiny show,
Through arid lands, their voices rise,
In desert's heart, 'neath starlit skies.

Ode to the night, a thorny croon,
An ancient tune, like some lost rune,
Their melodies, both sharp and sweet,
In harmony, the sands they greet.

Beneath the vast expanse they stand,
Guardians of the desert land,
Their spiny serenade resounds,
A timeless song in nature's bounds.

Encased in Spines

An ancient tree with bark of might,
A cloak of spikes in pale moonlight,
Guarding secrets, old insights,
Encased in spines, forever tight.

Beneath its shade, old tales around,
In whispered leaves, the words resound,
Of battles fought on sacred ground,
Through countless years in silence bound.

It stands as fortress, leaf and limb,
Each needle sharp, each branch so grim,
A sentinel where shadows swim,
With nature's hymn, it guards the rim.

Guardian Quills

Sharp and steady, fearless form,
Against the winds, against the storm,
Silent guard, in dusk or morn,
With quills like swords, they stand and warn.

With each defense, a story told,
Of how they stood so brave, so bold,
Their legacy, through ages old,
In quills that gleam with truths untold.

No foe can breach their prickly wall,
No intruder can make them fall,
They stand as one, so proud and tall,
Guardian quills, to heed the call.

Thorn-laced Symphony

In forests deep, where shadows play,
A symphony of thorns holds sway,
Each prick a note that leads the way,
Through ancient tunes, by night and day.

Strings of bramble, song of vine,
A melody both fierce and fine,
With every twist, a sound divine,
A thorn-laced symphony in line.

Harmonies in minor key,
Of nature's harshest, wild decree,
Yet beauty in its harsh decree,
A thorn-laced symphony so free.

Armored Quietude

Beneath the stars, in quiet night,
A creature wraps in armored might,
In stillness, hidden from our sight,
In armored quietude, forthright.

Each scale a silent watch it keeps,
Through dreams where ancient wisdom seeps,
In guarded silence, softly it sleeps,
Within the folds, where silence creeps.

Its cloak a testament to peace,
In quiet strength, it finds release,
And in this calm, the tensions cease,
Armored quietude's gentle lease.

Dances with Needles

In fields of green, she twirls around,
With needles sharp, the earth she found,
Her dance a silent, graceful fight,
Against the cloak of creeping night.

The moon a witness to her flight,
Shadows flit beneath the light,
In every stitch, a hope concealed,
In every turn, her strength revealed.

Her fingers weave, her fingers bind,
Embroidering the threads of mind,
The thorns that pricks, the petals sweet,
Her heartbeats match with every beat.

Defensive Elegance

Elegance in every stride,
In shadows where the secrets hide,
She guards her heart with silent grace,
A fortress in her gentle face.

Her words like silk, her mind a shield,
In every smile, a layer concealed,
She dances through the world's embrace,
A hidden star in endless space.

With every sway, a line she draws,
Protecting dreams without a pause,
Defensive elegance, her way,
Through nights and dawns, she holds the day.

The Surge of Spines

In verdant depths, the spines arise,
Defensive walls 'neath open skies,
They mark the boundaries firm and wide,
Where fragile hopes and fears collide.

The wind may hiss, the storm may drum,
Unyielding, they remain undone,
In every surge, a silent scream,
Of nature's strength within the dream.

Their armor speaks in whispering thorns,
Of battles fought, of victories worn,
Amidst the green, their stance aligns,
The steadfast surge, the surge of spines.

Silent Guardianship

Beneath the moon, in shadows deep,
Where secrets in the silence sleep,
The guardians stand with eyes so bright,
Through endless day and starry night.

No word they speak, no song they hum,
Yet all who pass, they do succumb,
To whispers carried in the breeze,
Of promises that never freeze.

In silent grace, they hold the line,
Against the tide of fateful time,
With watchful eyes, they guard the dream,
In twilight's glow, a constant beam.

Bristled Boundaries

Across the fields where shadows creep,
Bristled boundaries keep secrets deep.
Whispers weave through tangled vines,
Guarded tales of ancient lines.

In the dusk, the fences sigh,
Silent as the stars in sky.
Echoes of the past entwine,
Lips are sealed, yet hearts incline.

Through the hedgerows, breezes weave,
Silent truths on leaves they leave.
Borders drawn with steadfast hand,
Mark the line where secrets stand.

Shield of Silence

A fortress built of quiet calm,
A shield of silence, balm to balm.
In the hush of twilight's breath,
Find a peace beyond the death.

Silent walls of crystal air,
Guard the secrets held in care.
In the whisper of the night,
Echoes fade beyond the light.

Quiet reigns in solemn space,
Layered thick like velvet lace.
Underneath the starry dome,
Silent hearts can find their home.

Needlepoint Nights

Stars are stitched in night's embrace,
Needlepoint of time and space.
Threads of light in dark expanse,
Woven dreams in cosmic dance.

Every stitch a wish in bloom,
Hidden in the velvet gloom.
Patterns form and then dissolve,
Mysteries in stars revolve.

Silent seams in midnight's veil,
Crafted tales that stars unveil.
Needlepoint by moonlight's seam,
Bind the night with silver gleam.

Thorny Dance

Roses twirl in twilight's glow,
Thorny dance where secrets flow.
Petals whisper, steps entwine,
Nature's waltz in fluid line.

In the breeze, they weave and sway,
Casting shadows, light at bay.
Silent thorns in moonlit trance,
Join the roses in their dance.

In this ballet of dark and light,
Thorns embrace the petals tight.
Bound together, night advances,
In their timeless thorny dances.

Bristles and Balance

A dance upon a tightrope high,
With bristles sharp, against the sky.
Each step a wondrous, careful flight,
Between the dark and gleaming light.

In every move, a risk, a chance,
A fragile yet profound advance.
The balance tips, the winds may shear,
Yet firmest heart casts out its fear.

For life, it seems, a thread so thin,
On edges sharp where we begin.
The bristles prick, the balance sways,
In twilight's grace, the moment stays.

Hedge of Authority

A hedge stands tall, with leaves so dense,
A border strong, a firm defense.
Through branches thick, authority speaks,
In whispers loud, the silence peaks.

The roots dig deep, structurally sound,
Its boundaries held, dominion crowned.
Each leaf and thorn, a kingdom owns,
In ordered rows, the power known.

Yet beyond the hedge, the wild roams free,
A truth that borders cease to be.
Authority yields, but cannot confine,
The boundless spirit, the tangled vine.

Genteel Needles

Exquisite needles, crafted fine,
In pattern weave, a grand design.
Each stitch a tale, of grace and art,
A tender touch, a beating heart.

With every move, the threads align,
In hands so skilled, the cloth divine.
Genteel needles, with silent lore,
Embark on journeys unexplored.

Their whispered song, a lullaby,
In fabric's folds, the dreams comply.
To sew the soul, a thread so raw,
Genteel needles, the love they draw.

Prickly Poise

A cactus stands with poised intent,
In desert's breath, its testament.
Prickly guard, a silent bristle,
Yet blooms unfold, a gentle whistle.

Amidst the dry and arid space,
It's balance kept with quiet grace.
Through sun and stars, it finds its peace,
In solitude, its strength's release.

For even in the harshest clime,
A poise maintained, through endless time.
The prickly stance, a softened core,
In silent poise, the spirit soars.

Needle-clad Night

Starry skies in sable shroud,
Whisper secrets low and proud,
Moonlight through the pines so high,
Needles reach to touch the sky.

Shadows dance on forest floor,
Crickets chirp and night owls soar,
In the silence, nature's song,
Needle-clad, the night is strong.

Mist weaves through the ancient wood,
In this realm of calm and good,
Branches sway in night's embrace,
Needles cradle time and space.

Thorn Bearing Tides

Waves break upon the stony shore,
With a sound that's heard before,
Thorn bearing tides retreat and fight,
In the dance of day and night.

Salt and brine on breeze's edge,
Promises the sea will pledge,
Thorns of truth in waters grand,
Shaping dreams with shifting sand.

The ocean's heart beats strong and wild,
In its depths, a nature mild,
Tides that bear the thorn's embrace,
Craft a realm of boundless grace.

Prickly Wisdom

Elders speak by firelight's hue,
Wisdom shared with skies so blue,
Lessons clothed in prickly guise,
Guide us through the world's disguise.

Ancient words on wind's sweet breath,
Guard us from life's subtle depth,
In the prickly wisdom found,
Truths emerge where thoughts are bound.

Paths we walk with cautious stride,
With each thorn a noble guide,
Prickly wisdom in our soul,
Shapes our journey, makes us whole.

Barbed Ballet

Step by step in twilight's glow,
Barbed ballet begins to show,
Graceful movements, sharp and keen,
Echo through the charming scene.

Nature's dance with thorns in hand,
Mark each turn upon the land,
Barbs that sway in perfect time,
Craft a waltz of art, sublime.

Beauty in the harsh design,
Barbed ballet on life's fine line,
Twist and turn, a dance of might,
In the softness of the night.

Needled Peace

In deserts vast, where silence reigns,
Cacti stand with weathered grace.
Though sharp their spines to fend the pains,
They guard a tender, secret place.

A bloom unfolds in dusk's soft light,
A burst of color, fleeting, bright.
Against the odds, in harshest fight,
A symbol of enduring might.

The wind sings soft, a whispered tale,
Of resilience that will prevail.
Through drought and storm, and scorching gale,
The needled peace will never fail.

Spiky Sovereignty

Beneath the sun's relentless claim,
The cactus holds its realm with pride.
No softness here, no foothold tame,
　Its fortress stands, a thorny guide.

In arid lands where few dare tread,
Each spine a guard, each leaf a shield.
Resourceful roots in pathways spread,
　Defending life none can unyield.

A sovereignty in sharp array,
Yet blooms so rare in night display.
A reign of spines by night and day,
Proclaims the cactus here shall stay.

Embrace With Care

Amidst the sands where shadows weave,
The cactus stands in quiet flair.
A silent call for those who leave,
To find an embrace, but with care.

Its spines may warn of dangers near,
Yet deep within, life's essence glows.
For those who venture, drawing near,
A hidden heart each cactus shows.

In barren lands of trials shrewd,
A lesson in each spiny stair.
To seek the heart that's often viewed,
With caution in the driest air.

Sanctuary of Spines

In gardens wild with nature's hand,
A sanctuary of spines arise.
Defying drought through arid land,
A refuge where the spirit flies.

Each needle guards a story old,
Of battles won and hardships faced.
Within the spines, a heart of gold,
In every rib, resilience traced.

Among the thorns, a safe retreat,
A haven where the wild things grow.
In cacti's hold, life's rhythm beats,
A sanctuary in sun's warm glow.

Nocturnal Fortresses

Beneath the veil of silver light,
Ancient walls in silence stand,
Guardians of the endless night,
Their whispers brushed by twilight's hand.

Echoes through the moonlit keep,
Secrets old as crafted stone,
In shadowed halls where phantoms seep,
Stories linger, dark and lone.

Stars above like watchful eyes,
Glimmer through the soaring spires,
As the universe softly sighs,
Quiet dreams and deep desires.

Winds that kiss the castle cold,
Carry tales of yore and now,
In the stronghold's mystic hold,
Past and present both endow.

Time will fail to breach these gates,
Timeless, steadfast, they remain,
In their grip, the night abates,
Eternity their sole domain.

Bristled Stillness

In a grove where shadows play,
Branches whisper truths unseen,
Silent dances, night and day,
In a forest evergreen.

Leaves upon the ground are laid,
Carpets woven, so pristine,
Nature's breath in calm cascade,
Gracing paths of softened sheen.

Creatures nestled, feel the hush,
In the stillness of the morn,
Bearing witness as they brush,
Daybreak's silent, gentle born.

A melody of calm and ease,
Rides the cool, forsaken breeze,
Through the bristled arms of trees,
Where the moments never cease.

There among the sheltered stones,
Mysteries in quiet thrall,
Hear the earth's soft, whispered tones,
In the tranquil, timeless call.

Needles in Night

Under cobalt skies so deep,
Pine trees reach with needled hands,
In the forest, shadows sleep,
Wrapped in nature's tranquil bands.

Moonlight trickles through their spines,
Crafting patterns bold and slight,
Silent towers, ancient pines,
Guardians of the velvet night.

In the hush where owls glide,
Every echo seems more clear,
Near the brook where secrets hide,
Nighttime's whispers we can hear.

The air is crisp with starlit chill,
As the needles softly sway,
Every breath a gentle thrill,
In the twilight's somber play.

Paths of darkness, paths of light,
Weaving through the endless glade,
Needles in the heart of night,
Guide through dreams that slowly fade.

Shy Guardians

Amid the blooms that gently sway,
Butterflies in humble flight,
Guard the quiet of the day,
With wings that shimmer, pure and bright.

In the morning's dewy gold,
Hummingbirds with whispered grace,
Flit through moments that enfold,
The garden's peace in soft embrace.

Dragonflies on crystal streams,
Glide like spirits, light and fair,
Keep the balance of our dreams,
In their silent, watchful care.

Ladybugs with scarlet shields,
Walk among the blades of green,
Tend the blossoms, tend the fields,
Stealthy sentinels unseen.

Shy guardians within the wild,
Nature's keepers, small and true,
Through their quiet love compiled,
Harmony is born anew.

Prickly Silence

In the desert's quiet hold,
Sand and sun entwine their glow.
Cacti stand with whispers cold,
Guardians of the night they show.

Thorns defend their silent plea,
Guarded, stoic they remain.
In the night, the silence free,
Whispers heard in moonlit vein.

Nature's fortress, standing tall,
Echoes in the arid night.
Prickly shields, a silent call,
Desert bloom by starlight bright.

Quilled Boundaries

Across the rugged, endless span,
Cacti draw their quilled embrace.
Marking where the winds began,
In the quiet, verdant space.

Rigid boundaries hold their ground,
Roots dig deep, but spirits rise.
In the stillness, not a sound,
Stars reflect in ancient skies.

Quills define their guard so tight,
Yet within, a sense of grace.
Boundaries in the soft moonlight,
Nature's line, a gentle trace.

Embrace of Thorns

Through the parched and dusty plain,
Life endures in thorny hold.
Crimson blooms, their lives sustain,
Amidst a landscape fierce and bold.

Thorns like armor, layered thick,
Guard the treasure deep inside.
Nature's citadel, so slick,
In this harsh terrain, they bide.

In the twilight's gentle calm,
Shadows cast their stony kiss.
Thorns embrace, a desert psalm,
Firm and strong, yet full of bliss.

Guardians of Solitude

Stillness in the desert's breath,
Walls of thorns in cold repose.
Guardians in their timeless sheath,
Whispers in the wind disclose.

Solitude, their steadfast friend,
In the vast expanse, they thrive.
Silent watch, till journeys end,
Through the night, alone they strive.

Beneath the sun's relentless gaze,
Echoes of the past remain.
Guardians in the desert's maze,
Silent sentinels in pain.

Porcupine Reverie

In twilight's gentle, quiet haze,
A creature dreams of ancient days,
Soft whispers in the cool, dark maze,
With thoughts and dreams, it softly plays.

Quills that shimmer in the night,
A moonlit glow, a gentle light,
Through forest's silence, pure delight,
It dances free, devoid of fright.

Stars above like eyes so keen,
A world where only dreams convene,
Amongst the leaves, forever green,
In peaceful slumber, all is seen.

The forest breathes a lullaby,
A tranquil, soothing, midnight sky,
And in this still, the dreams won't die,
Through night they soar, they fly so high.

This reverie, a quiet gem,
In darkness, it becomes a realm,
Of porcupine's yearning helm,
A soft, enchanting, timeless hymn.

Silent Ascent

In silent steps, the night ascends,
A world where shadows long suspend,
A journey where the starlight bends,
In whispers, forest breath commends.

Through silent leaves, the path unfolds,
A tale beneath the moonlight told,
Each step a story gently molds,
In quiet, dreams of night behold.

Beneath the bough, the earth is still,
A calm that echoes nature's will,
The midnight air with subtle thrill,
A climb where only hearts can fill.

And in this silence, there's a song,
A melody that sings along,
A harmony where dreams belong,
In ascent, where echoes strong.

As night ascends in silent grace,
The stars align, their perfect space,
This journey, an eternal trace,
Through quiet, night's embrace.

Bristled Ballerina

A dance upon the forest floor,
Where bristled grace can't be ignored,
With every step, it moves once more,
In nature's quiet, gentle score.

A pirouette beneath the pine,
Where moonlit shadows intertwine,
A ballet rare, almost divine,
With quills that in the starlight shine.

Beneath the canopy so grand,
A solo dancer takes the stand,
With every twirl, we understand,
The beauty woven hand in hand.

In silence, it performs at night,
In darkness finds its pure delight,
The bristled queen of forest light,
A dancer hidden to our sight.

And through the night, it freely spins,
A ballerina with no sins,
In dreams where only night begins,
This dance of life, as silence wins.

Porcupine's Dance

The night unveils a gentle call,
Where shadows dance and leaves will fall,
A creature moves in twilight's thrall,
With steps that captivate us all.

Each quill a brush, with grace it paints,
A dance that every star acquaints,
Through forest glades, the night it faints,
In hypnotizing, fluid taints.

The dance begins with subtle rise,
Beneath the canopy's disguise,
In moonlit glow, where silence lies,
A mesmerizing, soft surprise.

And every step a story weaves,
Amongst the whispered, swaying leaves,
With heart and soul the night it cleaves,
This dance, eternal, never grieves.

In twilight's realm, it journeys far,
A dance beneath the dreamlit star,
A porcupine with no bizarre,
Transforms the night to its memoir.

Tender Guard

A whisper in the gentle breeze,
A song that dances through the trees,
Silent yet a firm embrace,
Protecting with an unseen grace.

In shadowed calm, it stands its ground,
With love so deep, no chain is bound,
A guard of tenderness, it stays,
Through moonlit nights and sunlit days.

Its armor forged of quiet care,
A shield of warmth in coldest air,
No battle fought, no blood to spill,
A heart's peace it guards, tranquil.

With every beat, it pulsates still,
Defender of the soul's goodwill,
A silent knight, unseen, unheard,
Guarding dreams with just one word.

The softest strength that e'er did shine,
A sacred vow, an ancient sign,
Protection in its truest form,
Safe within the heart's soft storm.

Delicate Fortresses

In petals soft as morning dew,
Lies strength unseen, and courage true,
Whispered walls of silent might,
Guarding dreams through darkest night.

A fortress built on tender ground,
Where melodies of life resound,
Each fragile leaf, a sentinel,
Standing watch through winter's chill.

With beauty as its steadfast shield,
A bastion where all wounds may heal,
Resilience in each rising bloom,
A sanctuary's gentle room.

No iron bars or stone decree,
But love's pure light, eternally,
These delicate fortresses stand,
An unseen force, a guiding hand.

In the garden of the heart,
They form the lines where worlds start,
Fragile yet enduring strong,
A haven where all souls belong.

Quilled Guardians

In twilight hues and shadows pale,
Quilled guardians weave their tale,
Of whispered truths and secrets kept,
Of promises in silence, slept.

Each quill, a word unsaid in time,
A sentinel of thoughts, sublime,
Protecting hearts from hurt and harm,
With unseen strength and quiet charm.

Their wisdom lives in every quirk,
In tender touch and subtle work,
Silent watchers of the night,
Guiding with a gentle light.

They harbor dreams in silent nests,
Guarding with their feathered vests,
A love described through every plume,
A comfort in the darkest room.

Quilled guardians, steadfast and true,
Hidden from the common view,
With every breeze they softly sway,
Protecting hearts in their own way.

Sharp Serenity

In fields where wildflowers grow,
Stands sharp serenity, aglow,
Shielded by the thorny spire,
Yet within, a heart's desire.

Each thorn a keeper of the peace,
Granting safety, pure release,
In their sharpness, calm resides,
In their presence, fear subsides.

A paradox of form and grace,
In every petal, soft embrace,
Where boundaries protect and hold,
A tranquil strength, a tale retold.

Serenity that's sharp, yet kind,
A union of the heart and mind,
Harmonious as nature's song,
Together they have stood so long.

In this sharp serenity's care,
Find a solace, pure and rare,
A haven where the soul can rest,
And dream in peace, forever blessed.

Subtle Defenses

Within the silence, shadows creep,
Whispers guard what secrets keep.
Beneath the moon's reflective sigh,
A fortress stands where echoes lie.

In twilight's grasp, defenses form,
Soft as morning, yet firm in storm.
Guardians, gentle, yet so strong,
Protect the heart, where dreams belong.

Veils unseen, yet ever there,
Layered shields of tender care.
No sword or spear can penetrate,
What love and wisdom consecrate.

Subtle whispers, walls of air,
Hide the soul, so tender, bare.
In every glance, a tale unfolds,
Of subtle strength that heart upholds.

When dawn arrives, defenses fade,
Yet remnants in the light cascade.
A soul untouched by night's cruel jest,
In gentle hands, it's softly blessed.

Mysterious Quills

In ancient tomes, the quills reside,
Mysteries in ink implied.
Fables told with every stroke,
Where dreams and reality softly cloak.

A scribe's enchantment in the night,
Drawing forth a world's delight.
Tales of wonder, myths revived,
In every line, a life contrived.

From feathered pen to parchment bare,
Visions dance in twilight's glare.
Stories whispered, secrets bound,
In quills, life's magic can be found.

Woven words in shadows glow,
Narratives of long ago.
Every quill a journey starts,
Through time and space, through minds and hearts.

Ethereal ink, a mystic thread,
Linking lives, the living and the dead.
Mysterious quills, forever penned,
In endless tales, they never end.

Prickled Fortitude

In rugged lands where cacti grow,
Resilience in the desert's glow.
Spines that guard with steadfast might,
Against the harshness, day and night.

Beneath the sun, where shadows thin,
Strength resides within the skin.
Prickled walls and hidden core,
A symbol strong forevermore.

The fiercest heat cannot betray,
The fortitude in nature's sway.
Against the odds, the cactus stands,
Defending life in arid sands.

Enduring trials where few would tread,
Surviving on what scant is fed.
A lesson in each thorny spear,
Of hope and courage year by year.

Prickled fortitude in silence speaks,
Of strength within the calm it seeks.
In every spine, a story told,
Of desert hearts, relentless, bold.

Guarded Whispers

In quiet corners, whispers dwell,
Guarding secrets none can tell.
Voices soft like morning mist,
Where shadows and the light exist.

Hushed tones weave around the heart,
Protecting truths from tearing apart.
Guarded whispers, softly veiled,
In their silence, stories hailed.

Shielded from the world's cruel jest,
In whispers, hearts find gentle rest.
A language few can understand,
In shadows drawn by tender hand.

Guardians of the fleeting breeze,
Whispers' touch brings subtle ease.
In every word that's softly voiced,
A hidden strength, profoundly poised.

When night descends and worlds grow still,
Whispers guard with iron will.
Promises in silence keep,
The heart's deep secrets, locked in sleep.

Nature's Armor

In forests deep, the bark stands tall,
Protecting life, one and all.
Roots spread wide in shadow's calm,
Nature's shield, a soothing balm.

Leaves of green, a shelter found,
Whispers soft, a tranquil sound.
Through storms they stand, embrace the fight,
Nature's armor, day and night.

Mountains rise with jagged crest,
A fortress strong, nature's best.
Rivers weave through valleys wide,
Guardians of life's ebbing tide.

Clouds above, a gentle shroud,
Whispers from the heavens loud.
Sunrise paints the world anew,
Nature's armor, strong and true.

Silent Spikes

Desert's edge where shadows fall,
Cacti stand, so green and tall.
Thorns they bear with silent grace,
Guardians of a quiet place.

Moonlight casts a silver hue,
Silent spikes in night's soft blue.
Whispers of the cool night breeze,
Through their spines, the silence frees.

Sunrise brings the dawn's first light,
Silent spikes bathe in the bright.
In the heat, they stand alone,
Guarding secrets, tales unknown.

With the stars, their watch they keep,
Silent spikes, as shadows creep.
Time moves on, yet they remain,
Silent guardians of the plain.

Guarded Heartbeats

Echoed steps in twilight glade,
Forest's hush, in green and shade.
Creatures whisper, heartbeats guard,
In nature's arms, never far.

Pine trees whisper secrets held,
Under moonlight's magic spell.
Heartbeats guarded, soft and low,
Through the forest's silent glow.

Night unfolds with gentle care,
Heartbeats linger in the air.
Stars above in velvet skies,
Guarded truths where silence lies.

Morning breaks with tender light,
Heartbeats warm and spirits bright.
Nature's pulse, a rhythm true,
Guarded heartbeats, me and you.

Spines of Solitude

In a realm where silence reigns,
Lonely spines through desert plains.
Cacti stand in solitude,
Guardians of nature's mood.

Whispers of a wind so still,
Secrets on the air they spill.
Solitude in spines so strong,
Echoed in the desert song.

Sunlight burns with fervent glare,
Solitude with tender care.
In their shadow, life does bide,
Spines of strength, a quiet guide.

Stars emerge in twilight's shroud,
Spines of solitude, unbowed.
Through the night they stand and wait,
Guardians at heaven's gate.

The Art of Distance

In shadows dwell the whispered breeze,
Where hearts remain apart with ease.
A tango forms, yet steps don't meet,
A dance performed by distant feet.

Eyes that glance but never touch,
Silent voices, saying much.
Bridges cross the silent streams,
In distance, we can keep our dreams.

Solitude, a painter's brush,
Crafts emotions in the hush.
Wide horizons, empty space,
Defines the art through subtle grace.

Echoes in the canyon deep,
Hold the secrets we can't keep.
Harmony in separate tunes,
Midnight sun and distant moons.

Paths that never intertwine,
Found in spaces so divine.
In the closeness, love may hide,
Yet distances our hearts can guide.

Spiked Symphony

In gardens, blooms a fierce array,
A symphony begins its play.
Notes of thorn and petal blend,
Melodies of hearts transcend.

Trumpets sound in bristled arch,
Horns of thistle making march.
Cactus needles, precise and keen,
Compose the sweetest unseen scene.

Roses whisper, orchids sigh,
Tulips hum a soft reply.
Carnations rise on upright stems,
Conducting nature's hidden gems.

The crescendo builds in prickly verse,
Harmony within the terse.
Silent notes on jagged strings,
In symphony, each thornbird sings.

Flower beds of jagged grace,
Spiking rhythms, curving space.
Through the wild, untamed refrain,
Beauty blooms in every pain.

Silent Porcupine

In forests deep, where shadows play,
A quiet soul has found its way.
With quills that guard and silence keep,
The porcupine in calm does seep.

Beneath the boughs of ancient pine,
Its stillness forms a gentle line.
Unmoved by rush of fleeting time,
It muses silently, sublime.

By moonlit glow, it stands alone,
A sentinel of sigh and stone.
Brambles whisper secrets near,
Yet porcupine has naught to fear.

Sharp defenses, soft inside,
Speaks a language dignified.
In silences and careful tread,
It teaches us where words have fled.

Patterns traced in fallen leaves,
Tales of silence, heart retrieves.
Porcupine, both guard and guide,
In quiet strength, it will abide.

Bristled Poise

Grace in thorns, a poised design,
Elegance in each define.
Bristles raised, not out of spite,
But beauty in defensive light.

Nature's fortress, clad in green,
Echoing a sovereign scene.
Porous armor, bending bark,
A stance both gentle and stark.

Porcupine with quills arrayed,
Shows a charm in light and shade.
Every movement, slow and sure,
In bristled poise, hearts endure.

Silent walks through forest paths,
Guarded by the spiny staffs.
Each step measured, soft and bright,
A portrait painted in the night.

In bristle's edge and calm reply,
Life's great lessons, soft and sly.
In poised defense, serene and mild,
We find the wisdom of the wild.

Quilled Quandary

In twilight's hush, the quills arise,
Beneath the moonlit, starry skies.
A dilemma sharp, with edge so fine,
In nature's hands, the stars align.

Shadows dance on forest floor,
Silent whispers, evermore.
Needles poised, a gentle threat,
A creature's armor, firmly set.

Questions twist in night's embrace,
Each spine a whisper, soft of grace.
A riddle wrapped in dusk's attire,
Enigmas born of nature's fire.

Protection donned in silent woe,
A quilled knight in evening's glow.
Pathways narrow, warnings clear,
In quilled quandary, facts appear.

Stillness holds a wary gleam,
In every spiked, reflective beam.
A puzzle faced in moon's own light,
Quills and night, forever tight.

Defense Mechanism

Armor gleams with pins and point,
Nature's dance, a sharp anoint.
Each needle guards the tender heart,
With every prick, it shows its art.

In the forest, shadows long,
A creature's shield, both firm and strong.
Silent in the night it prowls,
Defending peace, it softly growls.

Barriers raised against the night,
Sharper than the stars' own light.
Embedded deep, the instincts speak,
In each defense, the strong, the weak.

Guarded paths it treads alone,
Through the twilight, hears a moan.
Safety twined in bristled lines,
A testament in spiked designs.

Vigilance within each breath,
Shunning fear of threat and death.
Every spine a tale to tell,
Of life preserved in nature's swell.

Spiked Solace

Beneath the veil of twilight's glow,
A subtle peace begins to show.
With every quill, a story parts,
In spiked solace, nature starts.

Fields of green with spires so proud,
Silent whispers, never loud.
Each needle sings a tune so soft,
To calm the beast aloft, aloft.

Comfort found in armored grace,
A gentle hedge in forest's space.
Edges sharp, yet solace here,
In every quilled frontier.

Moonlight casts a silver thread,
On spiked repose, where dreams are led.
In night's embrace, the quills confide,
A solace found in spiky tide.

Through the dark, a lumined guide,
With pricks and pins, where fears reside.
In spiked solace, shadows wane,
Peace within the quilled domain.

Prickled Protection

Guardians of the twilight hour,
With prickles sharp, they wield their power.
Each thorn a promise, stout and true,
A barrier 'gainst the world's pursuit.

Silent sentinels by night,
Under moonsilver, bathed in light.
Protecting dreams in thistle crowns,
As darkness falls, the night surrounds.

Armor clad in nature's weave,
Each bristle warns what lies beneath.
In prickled stance, the night's defense,
A calm within, an outward fence.

In stillness, whispers softly stir,
With every spine, the air concurs.
A fortress built in nature's trust,
In prickled plains, the safe and just.

By day they rest, by night they rise,
With quilled embrace, they touch the skies.
A prickled protection, firm and wise,
Guarding life with watchful eyes.

Thorny Existence

In gardens where the wildflowers grow,
Thorns protect what none should know.
Guardians of petals, soft and sweet,
A harsh defense, yet bittersweet.

Beneath the rose, a hidden plight,
A prick to those who grasp too tight.
In life's embrace, a testament,
To hardships faced, and strength unbent.

Thorns may pierce and cause retreat,
Yet life's beauty lies beneath.
In every barb, a tale unfolds,
Of love and loss, both young and old.

Nature's wisdom, etched in pain,
Softness veiled in sharp refrain.
To hold the rose, endure the thorn,
For in that grasp, life's truths are born.

Thorny paths may carve the way,
But it's those scars that shape the day.
Hold the flower, brave the spines,
In thorny existence, one's strength aligns.

Porcupine's Prowess

In twilight's hush, they wander free,
A dance of quills beneath the tree.
Porcupine's steps, both soft and still,
A silent strength, a steadfast will.

Their armor constant, sharp and keen,
In moonlit woods, a shining sheen.
Defenders clad in nature's might,
A fortress in the darkened night.

Each quill a tale of battles past,
In every spike, a lesson cast.
Survival through the quiet veil,
A prickly quest, an ancient trail.

The forest whispers of their lore,
Of silent prowls and unseen roars.
In shadows deep, they guard their own,
A humble king on nature's throne.

Porcupine's prowess, sharp and stark,
A guardian of the forest's heart.
In every step, a world unseen,
Porcupine, the woodland's queen.

Warding Off the World

In bustling crowds and silent nights,
A shield of calm, the heart ignites.
Warding off the world's embrace,
To find serene, a sacred space.

Among the chaos, storms that rage,
A soul can craft a peaceful stage.
Guarded moments, fleeting still,
Sanctuary, by sheer will.

A wall of quiet, bricks of thought,
Inward journeys, solace sought.
The world denied, a breath reclaimed,
In solitude, life's pulse renamed.

Beyond the noise, a place to stand,
To ward off haste with gentle hands.
Within the heart, a fortress builds,
Where calm prevails, and silence fills.

Warding off the rushing tide,
A refuge found where dreams reside.
In solitude, a strength revealed,
To face the world, yet gently shield.

Serrated Shade

Beneath the canopy's embrace,
Where light and dark in fractals trace.
A serrated shade, both sharp and grand,
In shadows, secrets softly stand.

Leaves that cut, yet offer peace,
A paradox where fears release.
In whispers shared by ancient trees,
A language only silence sees.

The forest speaks in serried lines,
Of timeless tales in ageless rhymes.
Each serrated edge, a note so clear,
A song of life that all can hear.

In dappled lights, where shadows sway,
A dance of dark and bright ballet.
The serrated shade, a calming veil,
Where worries fade and hopes prevail.

In these woods, a haven found,
In serrated shadows, peace abounds.
Embrace the dark, yet know the light,
In shadowed depths, the soul takes flight.

Needle Veil

In the forest, whispers trail,
Through the shadows, frail and pale.
Silent secrets softly sail,
Wrapped within a needle veil.

Moonlight filters, silver, cold,
Touching needles, stories old.
Eerie echoes, truths unfold,
In the whispering, soft, and bold.

Branches sway, a latent gale,
Timeless woods, a needle veil.
Shadows dance, a hidden tale,
Nature's breath, a mystic scale.

In this place where spirits roam,
Needles weave a gentle home.
Paths untrodden, overgrown,
Veil of whispers, all alone.

Wanderers may pause and hail,
Mysteries in this quiet vale.
Through the fog and fern, so frail,
Guarded by a needle veil.

Fortress of Quills

Erected high on rugged hills,
A fortress strong, adorned with quills.
Guarding secrets, ancient, still,
In shadows deep, on quiet tills.

Wind howls past the stony face,
Quills stand guard, their timeless grace.
Echoes linger, fill the space,
In this fortress, a silent place.

Histories told in whispered shrills,
Guarded by the steadfast quills.
Time stands still, the air it chills,
Around this fortress, strong-willed.

Mystics, sages, spirits flow,
Where the secrets calmly grow.
Sentinels of long ago,
In the fortress, silent glow.

Legends deep, time distills,
Strong and quiet, the quills fulfill.
Mysteries that haunt our wills,
Within the fortress, high on hills.

Bristles of Caution

Paths untamed, with bristles bright,
Guarded fiercely, out of sight.
Caution whispers, in the night,
In the woodland's muted light.

Steps are measured, shadows cast,
Through the bristles, moving fast.
Caution's touch from ages past,
Guides us till the dawn's repast.

Nature's shield, a quiet plea,
Bristles whisper, wild and free.
Secrets of the forest sea,
Beneath the ancient, tangled tree.

In the thicket, caution sways,
Guarding paths of older days.
Holding back the wild's maze,
Whispered caution in its ways.

Through the bristles, soft and green,
Caution's hand lies crystal clean.
Paths we forge, seldom seen,
By the bristles' watchful sheen.

Quills and Quietude

In the stillness, deep and wide,
Quills stand silent, side by side.
Guardians of the quiet tide,
In their presence, peace presides.

Whispers lost in morning dew,
Quills stand watch, the world askew.
In the quietude, renewed,
Is the past that they construe.

Time and silence, intertwined,
Quills and quiet, hearts aligned.
In the stillness, peace we find,
Nature's secrets, well-defined.

Every breeze, a silent song,
In the quills, where they belong.
Quiet moments, pure and strong,
Harbor dreams not far along.

Quills and quietude, a pair,
Standing tall, beyond compare.
In the stillness, secrets share,
Nature's breath of tranquil air.

Poised in Defense

In twilight's waning, shadows blend,
Guardians rise, resolve won't bend.
Swift and silent, ever near,
Defenders of the realm appear.

With eyes that pierce the veil of night,
They stand against encroaching blight.
No respite do they seek or need,
On duty they shall ever heed.

Their vigilance, a steadfast bond,
Beyond the veil, beyond the beyond.
From dusk till dawn, in wary dance,
In darkness, they find their trance.

Against the storm, they hold the line,
With courage fierce, their spirits shine.
No fear shall breach their strong embrace,
Valor guards their sacred space.

In whispered legends, they'll remain,
The watchful few, who spare the pain.
For in the quiet, starlit drowse,
Poised in defense, they keep their vows.

Silent Shields

Beneath the moon, in silvered light,
Silent shields await the fight.
Their gleaming forms, a silent pact,
To safeguard dreams from fate's impact.

A wordless vow, unseen, unheard,
Their strength lies not in spoken word.
With silent grace, they weave their guard,
A timeless dance in night's backyard.

Through battles fought and battles won,
They hold their stance until the sun.
Against the tide of darkened fears,
Their silent shields repel the tears.

No trumpet calls to mark their deed,
Yet heroes rise in times of need.
Their silent valor, pure and bold,
In shadows, their brave hearts unfold.

Thus in the night, when quiet holds,
Their presence looms, a story told.
Of silent shields that guard the soul,
An unseen force, they make us whole.

Silent Quills

In solitude, the quills reside,
Their silent song in ink they hide.
With gentle strokes, they weave the tale,
Of dreams set free on parchment's sail.

A quiet hush within the night,
Their words take wing, a silent flight.
No need for voice to share the dream,
They whisper truths in twilight's gleam.

With every line, a world unfolds,
A tapestry of hearts and souls.
The quills, though still, their power vast,
In silence, they record the past.

They capture moments, soft and grand,
With deft precision, hand in hand.
Their silent touch on waiting sheets,
Gives life to tales, old souls it greets.

Thus, silent quills, in shadows bide,
Their stories told 'neath starry tide.
In written whispers, dreams do spill,
The silent quills remain, until.

Embrace with Thorns

In gardens wild, the roses bloom,
Amidst their beauty, shadows loom.
Their petals soft, with colors bright,
Yet thorns await in hidden light.

An embrace so sweet, it draws you near,
But heed the thorns, their presence clear.
For in their clasp, a price they ask,
A silent test in beauty's mask.

With tender care and mindful grace,
Navigate their fierce embrace.
For in their thorns, a lesson lies,
Of strength and fragility tied.

A paradox of gentle might,
These roses bloom in day and night.
Their thorns, a guard, their blooms, a gift,
In balance, both our spirits lift.

So in their midst, we find our way,
In thorns and petals, we shall stay.
Embrace the rose, but with respect,
For thorns protect what we neglect.

Nature's Currency

Leaves of gold dance high and low,
Rustling secrets only they know.
In sunlight's kiss, they gently sway,
A verdant wealth that won't decay.

Whispering winds through boughs entwine,
Nature's wealth, an ancient sign.
Pantries filled with autumn's hue,
A treasure chest of morning dew.

Golden dawns and sapphire seas,
Riches of the forest, roots, and trees.
Mountains cloaked in velvet mist,
Each raindrop, a diamond kissed.

Songs of earth in verdant notes,
Wealth in petals, poems, and coats.
Nature's vault, no lock, no key,
A legacy for you and me.

Fields of green, skies of blue,
Gems of truth in every hue.
In nature's purse, abundance grows,
Her currency, the world bestows.

Spined Elegance

In silhouette, the hedgehog glides,
On nimble legs, through dusk it hides.
By moonlit path, it softly treads,
A prickly crown upon its head.

With nature's armor, it stands tall,
Each spine a sentinel if called.
Against the world it firmly braces,
A gentle heart in silent places.

Soft eyes glisten in the night,
Untamed, unseen in dim twilight.
A humble knight in earthen shades,
In woodland realms where silence fades.

Tales of old, and whispered lore,
Of spined elegance, we adore.
In dreams it wanders, unafraid,
A sovereign of the forest glade.

Grace in stride, and strength within,
A creature wrapped in nature's skin.
Where shadows play and night descends,
The hedgehog roams, our quiet friend.

Whispering Barbs

In desert lands where shadows fall,
A cactus stands, serene and tall.
Its silent whispers tell a tale,
Of arid winds and twilight's veil.

Barbed with secrets, clad in green,
A fortress in the barren scene.
Each spine, a guardian of its grace,
In vast expanse, it finds its place.

Blossoms rare as morning's yawn,
Breathe life anew by break of dawn.
From barbs emerge, a bloom's delight,
A fleeting kiss of color's light.

In stillness of the twilight zone,
Its whispers call to those alone.
A tale of strength, of time's embrace,
In quiet lands, a stalwart face.

Desert's watchful sage and guide,
With brooding spines, it stands with pride.
A symbol of the scars we bear,
In silent strength, we're all laid bare.

A Quill's Refuge

Nestled in the broken bark,
A porcupine, so calm and stark.
In quills of black and white it sleeps,
Secrets of the night it keeps.

Silent guardian of the pines,
In moonlit shroud, with tender spines.
Beneath its coat, a tranquil heart,
A creature set in world apart.

With cautious steps it roams the land,
A quill's refuge 'mid shadows stand.
In every spine, a story's thread,
Of woods it calls its homestead.

Trees will whisper, winds will sigh,
With gentle rustle, as they cry.
The forest hugs this gentle shield,
In solitude, its wounds are healed.

In nature's arms, it softly treads,
With peaceful thoughts in gently beds.
A porcupine's serene embrace,
In quill's refuge, finds its place.

Elegance in Armor

In twilight's gentle grace, they gleam,
Shields of silver, a noble dream.
Silent warriors of the dusk,
With polished shells, they quietly trust.

Glistening in the night so pure,
Their stance is poised, their hearts demure.
Strength concealed in beauty's cloak,
In armored elegance, they evoke.

Beneath the stars, they guard the field,
A fortress' strength, no sword to wield.
Mystery in midnight's glow,
A silent grandeur that they show.

In stillness, they command the space,
With dignity, they hold their place.
A silent dance of shadowed art,
In armored grace, they light the dark.

Elegance in form and fight,
A tranquil force beneath the night.
With armored peace, they softly sway,
Silent sentries till the break of day.

Watchful Spines

Guardians of the desert's sweep,
Prickly sentinels that vigil keep.
Steadfast in the arid land,
A watchful eye on shifting sand.

Green crowns in the blazing sun,
Together yet alone, as one.
Their spines a fortress none break through,
In silent strength, they rule the view.

Rooted deep in harsh terrain,
They drink the sky, they drink the rain.
Ancient watchers of the dry,
Their arms embrace the endless sky.

Prickled skin and standing tall,
Witness to the night's cool sprawl.
Soft whispers in the cactus grove,
Stories of the old winds they rove.

With spiked defense, they guard the peace,
Incarnate strength that will not cease.
In sunset's hue, they take their throne,
Silent keepers of a land unknown.

The Cautious Quill

Delicate beneath the sky,
A cautious quill, afraid to fly.
In whispered winds, it finds its keep,
A poet's heart in silence deep.

Beneath the trees, in shadows soft,
It pens with care, in lettering oft.
Each stroke a careful, gentle line,
A cautious heart in brightness shine.

Quiet muse of hidden thought,
With every line, a truth is sought.
In stillness of the evening's hush,
A world unveiled, a modest brush.

Soft echoes in the night it hears,
A tale of dreams, a form of fears.
And though it trembles, there it stands,
A cautious quill in trembling hands.

In careful script, it weaves a spell,
A parchment tale, where stories dwell.
With every line, a world to fill,
In gentle ink, the cautious quill.

Silent Barbs

In shadows dark, where secrets sleep,
Silent barbs their vigil keep.
Guardians of the still night air,
In twilight's cloak, they nestle there.

Whispered winds through thickets weave,
Where silent barbs in darkness grieve.
Unseen defenders of the night,
A thorny presence out of sight.

No word they speak, no sound they make,
In silent realms, their place they stake.
Shadowed figures cloaked in mist,
With guarded strength, they do persist.

Through the night, their whispers roam,
In silent barbs, they find their home.
A storied strength in whispered seams,
Their silence guards the land of dreams.

In moonlit glow, they stand so still,
With silent barbs, they shape the hill.
Invisible yet always near,
The night's soft breath, they softly hear.

Lonesome Protector

In shadows tall, he stands alone,
With bark and brawn, with roots unknown,
A guardian of forest deep,
A vigil firm, his secrets keep.

Through seasons' dance, through time's cruel jest,
He shelters life within his crest,
Yet solitude, his closest kin,
No comfort found, no warmth within.

The wind may howl, the storm may rage,
He braves it all, age after age,
A silent knight, with crown of green,
Defender of a silent scene.

So stand we all, in night or day,
A lonesome path, a guiding way,
Protector born, though hearts may ache,
In solitude, our strength we take.

As dawn awakes, as dusk descends,
His timeless watch, it never ends,
In whispers soft, the forest cheers,
To Lonesome Protector, through the years.

Quilled Harmony

Beneath a sky of cobalt blue,
A symphony of shades and hues,
The quills of life, so deftly spun,
A tapestry of light begun.

In finest threads, the stories weave,
Of joy and pain, of give and leave,
A harmony, in gentle sway,
Echoes soft, by night or day.

Each note a tale, each chord a dream,
In concert with the river's gleam,
The whispered winds a sweet refrain,
A quilled ballet of sun and rain.

As twilight spills its crimson glow,
A serenade, both high and low,
The looms of fate, they hum with grace,
In quilled harmony, we find our place.

In heart and soul, in mind and pen,
We quilt the world, again, again,
A symphony, both wild and free,
Is found in quilled harmony.

Silent Strengths

In quiet gaze, the world observes,
A silent strength, no need for words,
In subtle acts, in whispers low,
A might is found, a steady flow.

The calm of dawn, the hush of night,
In shadows deep, in gentle light,
A strength resides, unseen, profound,
In voiceless vow, in silent sound.

Through raging storm, through bitter cold,
Silent strengths, they take their hold,
In every heart, a power lies,
Beyond the reach of spoken ties.

So stand the mountains, tall and grand,
In quiet pride, they firmly stand,
A testament to inner might,
In stillness bold, they face the night.

In life, we find, with every breath,
Silent strengths that conquer death,
In silence, there is strength anew,
A force unseen, yet steadfast, true.

Spiked Solitude

In spiked embrace, the lone one stands,
Amidst the shifting desert sands,
With thorns that guard from closer glance,
He dances in a silent trance.

The sun above, his closest friend,
Together, through the seasons bend,
In solitude, he finds his peace,
A sanctuary, where thoughts release.

With every spike, a tale untold,
Of battles won, of nights so cold,
In solitary strength, he blooms,
A striking form, midst desert rooms.

The moonlight casts a silver shade,
On spiked solitude, so unafraid,
A sentinel of arid land,
He lingers, still and bravely grand.

For in the quiet and the calm,
He finds a strength, a healing balm,
In spiked solitude, he grows,
An emblem of the strength life shows.

The Protective Dance

Under skies, the shadows prance,
With veils of night, in a silent trance.
Guardians of the dim-lit night,
In armor gleams, a valiant fight.

In circles round, the spirits spin,
To ward away the doubts within.
Their movements, fluid as a dream,
Defend the heart from fears unseen.

Beneath the stars, their effort shines,
A careful weave of ancient signs.
They dance to shield, to safeguard light,
Through twilight hours, till morning's sight.

Each step a vow to keep the peace,
Unseen, their vigilance won't cease.
In shadows deep, their grace is found,
A dance to keep both safe and sound.

With dawn's approach, they start to fade,
Yet their essence in hearts is laid.
A timeless waltz, protectors true,
In every dusk, their dance renew.

Tender Like Thorns

In gardens where the roses bloom,
A dance of red dispels the gloom.
Amidst the beauty, thorns appear,
Both soft caress and hidden spear.

Fragile blooms in morning dew,
Hold mysteries in colors' view.
Their petals whisper love's embrace,
Yet warn of thorns in gentle grace.

A touch so soft, yet caution speaks,
For tenderness is not for the weak.
In every tear, a lesson grows,
From pain, the beauty sharply flows.

Love's essence, wrapped in thorny guise,
Conceals the truth in lovers' eyes.
With every touch, both joy and pain,
A dance that hearts will long remain.

In twilight's hush, the roses stand,
A testament to love's command.
Tender like thorns, the heart's refrain,
To bloom, to ache, to feel again.

A Quill's Wisdom

Upon the parchment, stories spill,
From feathered tip, the quill stands still.
In ink profound, it whispers lore,
Of ages past and futures' shore.

Wisdom flows from crafted lines,
A tapestry of thoughts entwines.
Each stroke a mirror, deep and wide,
Reflects the worlds within untried.

With every dip in inkwell's pool,
The quill becomes the sage's tool.
In silence speaks, with grace and art,
To pen the secrets of the heart.

Ancient tales in prose unfold,
A quill's embrace, both firm and bold.
Its wisdom echoes through the page,
A timeless voice from age to age.

In quiet hours, the quill remains,
A guardian of written strains.
With ink and thought, it paints the air,
A vessel for the soul's repair.

Barbed Embrace

Amid the thorns, a rose is found,
Its beauty in the harsh profound.
A paradox of love and sting,
Wrapped tight within its thorny ring.

The heart, like petals, soft and pure,
Finds strength in every prick, endure.
Each barbed embrace, a lesson taught,
In pain, resilience, fiercely wrought.

In moments of the deepest night,
The thorns protect, yet hold so tight.
A love that's fierce, both shield and chain,
In barbed embrace, we learn to reign.

Through trials harsh, the soul will bloom,
As roses rise from earthen tomb.
In every thorn, a challenge met,
A boundless beauty we won't forget.

So hold the rose, though thorns may press,
In barbed embrace, we find finesse.
For love demands a heart that's brave,
To cherish both the thorns and wave.

Wary Whispers

In the twilight's gentle shade,
Softly tread the paths we've made,
Silent echoes, none invade,
Wary whispers, dreams cascade.

Moonlight's veil on secrets kept,
Through the night, the shadows crept,
Timid voices barely wept,
In the calm, our fears adept.

Hidden words in night's cool air,
Secrets tangled in despair,
Wary whispers everywhere,
Speak of hopes and hearts laid bare.

Starry skies and whispered dreams,
Truths unravel at the seams,
Silent partners, moon's pale beams,
Guide us through these fragile themes.

Every secret softly told,
In the dark, our hearts unfold,
Wary whispers, brave and bold,
Tales of truths and fears retold.

Nature's Sentinel

Standing tall, through sun and rain,
Guardians of each wild plain,
Winds and whispers they contain,
Nature's sentinel, sustain.

Branches bend but do not break,
Silent watch they undertake,
Every dawn, a vow they make,
Holding fast for nature's sake.

In their shadows, calm prevails,
Stories told by rustling veils,
Marking time through endless trails,
Wise and true as morning sails.

Canopies that kiss the sky,
Shelter where the small ones lie,
Nature's sentinel stands nigh,
Ever vigilant, their cry.

Whispers woven through their leaves,
Mysteries each heart believes,
Nature's sentinel retrieves,
Ancient tales the earth receives.

Spiny Embrace

In the desert's silent grace,
Hides a friend with spiny face,
Arms that gather, slow embrace,
In their hold, a guarded space.

Nature's armor, thorny shield,
Survival's secrets they reveal,
In their spiny grasp, concealed,
Hidden strength, unyielding, sealed.

Through the winds and scorching sun,
Fields of cacti, battles won,
Each embrace a tale begun,
Of the earth and struggles spun.

In the night, their shadows cast,
Forms that speak of ages past,
Spiny embrace, holding fast,
Stories from the first to last.

Time and tale within their hold,
Legends of the desert told,
Spiny embrace, calm and bold,
Nature's grasp, an art to mold.

Thorned Tranquility

In the meadow's gentle rise,
Thorns conceal with no disguise,
Peaceful whispers, nature's lies,
Thorned tranquility defies.

Silent guardians of the bloom,
Hidden strength within their gloom,
Petals' scent where thorns consume,
Breathe the air of sweet perfume.

Every thorn, a watchful guide,
Peace and peril side by side,
In their midst, where hearts confide,
Thorned tranquility abides.

Within shadows, secrets blend,
Calm and chaos, both defend,
In their thorns, beginnings end,
Harmony they safeguard, send.

Tranquil blooms with thorned embrace,
Balance forged in wild's face,
Every thorn a calm retrace,
In their guard, a gentle grace.

The Spine's Pact

In shadows deep, the spine stands tall,
A sentinel for body's call.
Each vertebra, a soldier bold,
In life's great dance, both young and old.

A covenant of strength and might,
Under the moon's soft silver light.
Through trials rough and burdens vast,
The spine endures, steadfast.

In every twist and every bend,
A loyal guardian, a silent friend.
From dawn's first light to twilight's glow,
In steadfast duty, it does go.

Our trials it carries, our dreams it holds,
A tale of resilience, silently unfolds.
Bound in sinew, bone, and grace,
A warrior's heart in life's embrace.

So honor the spine, the unseen knight,
Guardian of our days and night.
In upright stance or restful sleep,
Its vigil, ceaseless, it does keep.

Quiet Vigilance

In silence, watch the world unfold,
A tale of patience, quiet and bold.
A sentinel in shadows cast,
Guarding moments, fleeting fast.

Under moonlight's tender gaze,
Through trouble's dark and winding maze.
A steadfast watcher, calm and still,
Awaiting dawn's first gentle thrill.

Endurance in the whispered night,
Alert in gloom, shunning fright.
An essence cloaked in dark and light,
Keeping vigil, till morning bright.

In stillness, strength is often found,
A quiet guard, without a sound.
Through tempests wild, through calm seas,
A silent oath to stillness please.

So let us honor the quiet guard,
A role profound, though often marred.
In peace and strife, in joy and pain,
In quiet vigilance, we sustain.

Defensive Brilliance

In the throes of battle's heat,
A mind as sharp as razor's fleet.
Defensive brilliance, quick and keen,
In every move, strategy seen.

Footsteps whisper on frozen ground,
Where, amidst chaos, wisdom's found.
A parry here, a dodge so swift,
Guardianship with deftness, gift.

Under pressure's steel embrace,
Each decision, measured pace.
A game of wits, a dance of blades,
Through tumultuous wars and dark parades.

In steadfast heart and eagle's eye,
Defensive brilliance shall never die.
From shadows weave a guardian's cloak,
Against life's blows, their stance provoke.

So hail the mind, resilient and bright,
In darkest times, it finds the light.
For in defensive arts, brilliance lies,
A beacon under stormy skies.

Spikes in Silence

Beneath the moon's soft, silver gleam,
Lie secrets that the night redeems.
In atlas' graveyard, shadows dance,
Upon the armor's sharp expanse.

Spikes in silence, fierce and cold,
In moments lost, their stories told.
Aguard in twilight's gentle fold,
Their presence felt, though often bold.

In quietude, their wisdom speaks,
Of strength found not in loudest creeks.
Like sentinels in shadows deep,
Their counsel in the silence keep.

Each spike a sentinel of pride,
In stillness, might and fears collide.
A testament to strength unseen,
In muted realms where shadows lean.

So honor those in silence clad,
Defenders strong where peace is glad.
In echoes of the quiet night,
Spikes guard on with silent might.

Barbs of Wisdom

In fields where wildflowers swing,
Wisdom's barbs are hidden there,
Sharp to touch in seasons spring,
Piercing truths beyond compare.

Roots entangle time and lore,
Whispers through the leaves intone,
Echoes of the ancient score,
In each thorn a truth is sown.

Petals soft with scented grace,
Hide the thistle's slight embrace,
Where the seeker sees its face,
Barbs of wisdom interlace.

Pain and beauty intertwined,
Nature's secrets all aligned,
Through the briar what we find,
Knowledge tender, sharply kind.

Embrace the sting and feel the growth,
In life's garden, wisdom both,
Cling to petals, learn from thorn,
Through each barb a soul reborn.

Nocturnal Sentinels

Underneath the moon's soft light,
Shadows cross the silent night,
Sentinels in dark array,
Guard the secrets of the day.

Owls whisper ancient rhymes,
Through the branches, across the times,
Their eyes, glowing silent fire,
Embers of a dark desire.

Bats in whispers, wings in flight,
Dance with stars, consume the night,
Echoes of a world unseen,
Woven in a midnight dream.

Wolves' howls pierce the tranquil air,
Songs of sorrow, songs of care,
Through the forest, spirits tread,
Binding life with unseen thread.

Silent watchers, cloaked in dark,
Bearers of a midnight spark,
Holding vigil, through the gloom,
Guardians of night's near tomb.

Quilled Echoes

In the still of silent grove,
Porcupine with cautious move,
Quills like whispers in the air,
Echoing a watchful care.

Rustling leaves beneath the moon,
Nature hums a quiet tune,
Every step leaves marks unshown,
In the night, they walk alone.

Quills that guard with gentle might,
Defend the heart throughout the night,
Soft beneath the armored skin,
A silent strength that lies within.

Voices lost in verdant sea,
Quilled echoes of the forest free,
A dance of caution, dance of grace,
In the dark, they find their place.

Guardians of the shadows deep,
Secrets of the woods they keep,
Whispered truths in quilled repose,
Echoes where the wild grows.

The Tender Spine

Through the meadow, winds they weave,
Stories that the willows leave,
In their sway, a tale unfolds,
Tender spine of nature holds.

Branches bend with gentle care,
Stretching fingers through the air,
Every leaf a softer side,
In their dance, they will not hide.

Beneath the bark, a strength unseen,
In each ring, a life serene,
Soft the leaf and strong the branch,
In their unity, they stanch.

From the roots to skyward climb,
Echoes of the ageless time,
In their shade, a soul can find,
Solace of the tender spine.

Whispers through the valley floor,
Comfort in the winds that roar,
In their grace, a strength defined,
Nature's heart, the tender spine.

Bristled Secrets

In shadows thick, where whispers roam,
Lies a secret, wrapped in foam.
Bristled whispers, urgent plea,
Underneath the old oak tree.

Mystic winds through branches maze,
Conceal secrets, tangled haze.
Ancient roots and silent guide,
Where the unseen truths reside.

In the night's enshrouded veil,
Mysteries in bristles trail.
Hidden echoes, shadows speak,
Wisdom, fragile, old and weak.

Through the whispers one might seek,
Revelations, mild yet bleak.
In the dark they softly play,
Bristled secrets' wordless lay.

As the dawn begins to wake,
Shadows slowly now forsake.
Secrets in the daylight cling,
Whispered words the night did bring.

Pinnacle of Thorns

Upon the crest where roses weep,
Lies the thorn where none dare sleep.
Scarlet petals, soft they mourn,
Near the pinnacle of thorn.

Beauty sprawls but guarded keen,
Pricked by what lay in-between.
Fragrant whispers of the bold,
Wrapped in courage, stories told.

In the garden, shadows dance,
Thorns protect at first glance.
Guardians of the fragile bloom,
Spiraled thorns in muted gloom.

High above, the thorns present,
Peaks of trials, no relent.
Strength and grace, a mirrored pair,
Pinnacle of thorns declare.

Though the path be lined in grief,
Blooms hold fast to their belief.
Roses climb with tempered grace,
Pinnacle of thorns they chase.

Nature's Defense

In fields where wildflowers sprawl,
Nature stands with sturdy call.
Defense in every blade of grass,
Guarding life as ages pass.

Tiny creatures make their stand,
Each within the great command.
Symbiosis, life in pact,
Nature's trust, a sacred act.

Mountains rise with jagged shield,
Forests dense their knowledge yield.
From the crosswinds to the earth,
Every form has priceless worth.

Waters flow with soothing grace,
Hold their secrets, vast embrace.
Tides and rivers, currents blend,
Nature's flow, a constant friend.

From the sky to ocean floor,
Nature guards her boundless shore.
All of life she will defend,
Nature's balance, no amend.

Milton Keynes UK
Ingram Content Group UK Ltd.
UKHW020628170824
447045UK00011B/595

9 789916 864241